Aug. '89
For our young friend,
Cerissa —

We love you,
Glin Tata Keysha & Jesse

Cerissa Ballard
~~663-3859~~
~~Address~~
~~9210 Linda~~
~~Sherry~~
~~WY~~

840-2684

MY FIRST
BOOK OF
BIBLE
STORIES

This edition © Ward Lock Limited
1988

First published in the U.S.
in MCMLXXXVIII by Ideals
Publishing Corporation,
Nashville, Tennessee.

ISBN 0-8249-8265-7

Printed and bound in Czechoslovakia

MY FIRST
BOOK OF
BIBLE
STORIES

Illustrated by Harry G. Theaker

IDEALS CHILDREN'S BOOKS
Nashville, Tennessee

CONTENTS

OLD TESTAMENT

THE GARDEN OF EDEN

In the beginning, God created heaven and earth. There was no light, so God created light. He called the light day and the darkness night. He created the seas, the land, grass, flowers, and trees. He made the sun, the moon, the stars, all the animals and birds, the whales, the fish, and all the other creatures that live in the sea.

Then he created a man and a woman. He called the man Adam and the woman Eve. He made a wonderful garden for them to live in called the Garden of Eden. It was full of beautiful trees.

Two of them were very special trees. One was the Tree of Life that stood in the middle of the garden, the other was the Tree of Knowledge of Good and Evil.

God had forbidden Adam and Eve to eat

the fruit of this tree. They were glad to obey God because they were so happy in the beautiful garden.

One day, Eve was admiring the Tree of Knowledge of Good and Evil when a huge snake slithered next to her.

"The fruit looks good, doesn't it?" said the snake. "Why not eat some?"

"Oh, I couldn't," said Eve. "God has forbidden it. If I do, I will die."

"Surely you don't believe that," said the snake, its clever little eyes gleaming wickedly. "God only said that because he knows that if you eat the fruit, you will know all about good and evil and be as powerful as he is. You will be like a god yourself."

Eve gazed at the fruit again. It looked very tempting. If she ate it, perhaps she would become clever and wise, so she ate some of the fruit and gave some to Adam too.

As soon as they had eaten it, they knew

they had done wrong and they hid themselves from God. But God knew that they had eaten the fruit and he was so angry with Adam and Eve, that he made them leave the beautiful garden forever.

He set angels with a flaming sword to guard the Tree of Life, so that Adam and Eve could not eat its fruit and know the secret of how to live forever.

NOAH'S ARK

Long ago, the people on earth were so wicked that God sent a flood to destroy them. God saved one man called Noah because he was good. "Noah," said God, "build an ark, a house boat, for your family and take on board two of every living creature on earth. If you do this, your family and these creatures will be kept alive."

Noah obeyed God. Then the rain came down and the water rose, covering the top of the highest mountain. Everything was destroyed except the people and animals in the ark, which floated on the flood.

At last the rain stopped; Noah opened a window and set free a dove. She returned with an olive twig in her beak, so Noah knew that the flood had gone down. God had kept his promise and saved everyone in the ark.

THE STORY OF JOSEPH

Jacob was an old man when his two youngest sons, Joseph and Benjamin, were born. Jacob had 12 sons altogether, but he loved Joseph the best and gave him a magnificent coat. Joseph's older brothers were extremely jealous of him and when Joseph dreamed that they would bow down to him one day, they hated him even more.

One day, Jacob sent Joseph to see his brothers, who were looking after their sheep a short journey from home. When the brothers saw him, they felt like killing him; instead, they took his beautiful coat and threw Joseph into a pit.

Later, they pulled him out and sold him as a slave. They smeared the beautiful coat with goat's blood so that Jacob would think his son had been killed by wild beasts.

Years passed. Joseph was no longer a slave, but a friend and adviser to Pharaoh, King of Egypt. He understood all Pharaoh's dreams and had told him of years of good harvest followed by years of famine.

There was also famine in Jacob's country. He sent all his sons, except Benjamin, to buy corn from Pharaoh, who had plenty because Joseph had warned him to store it. When they reached Egypt they were brought before Joseph. They bowed before the rich man, but did not recognize him.

Joseph recognized them and accused them of being spies. He told them that they must return with Benjamin; then he would believe their story. He kept one brother prisoner and allowed the others to leave with sacks of corn.

They returned to buy corn again and brought Benjamin with them. Joseph was thrilled to see him. When the brothers left, Joseph hid his silver cup in the top of

Benjamin's corn sack. Then he sent his servants after them, accusing them of stealing his cup.

The anxious brothers were brought back. Joseph couldn't pretend any longer. He sent all his servants away and told his brothers who he really was. They could, hardly believe that this rich and powerful Egyptian was their brother.

Joseph sent them to fetch his father Jacob, who was overjoyed to see the son he thought was dead, alive and well.

MOSES FREES THE ISRAELITES

Long ago, Pharaoh, King of Egypt, made the people of Israel slaves. The Israelites worked hard and were badly treated so Pharaoh was afraid that one day they would rebel and kill the Egyptians. To prevent this he ordered all baby boys born to Israelites to be thrown into the River Nile.

One of the Israelite women hid her baby in a basket of bulrushes, and floated it among the river reeds.

Pharaoh's daughter came down to the water and found the basket. When the baby inside cried, the Princess felt very sorry for him and decided to keep him. She called him Moses.

Moses grew up as a prince, but he did not forget that he was an Israelite. He saw how terrible their life was. One day, he killed an

Egyptian who was beating an Israelite slave.

Moses fled to another country where God spoke to him: "I will send you to Pharaoh to free my people, the Israelites, from slavery."

Moses returned to Egypt with his brother Aaron and they asked Pharaoh to free the Israelites. Pharaoh laughed and asked them for a sign of their god. Aaron threw down the rod he was carrying and it turned into a snake. But all Pharaoh's magicians did the same. Aaron's snake swallowed all the others, but still Pharaoh refused.

So, through Moses, God sent terrible plagues to Egypt: rivers of blood, frogs, lice, flies, dead cattle, hail, locusts, and darkness. Finally, he killed all the firstborn Egyptian sons, including Pharaoh's son. At last, Pharaoh agreed to free the Israelites.

Young and old, the Israelites followed Moses into the desert with all their animals. God led them with a pillar of cloud by day

and a pillar of fire by night.

Pharaoh broke his promise and chased after them with all his chariots. The Israelites were trapped by the Red Sea, but God divided the water and made a path through the sea for them to walk through, a wall of water on either side.

Pharaoh followed, but God rolled the waves back over him, and he and all his soldiers drowned. The Israelites, led by Moses, escaped.

DAVID
THE SHEPHERD BOY KING

There was once a shepherd boy called David who became a king. David had seven brothers who were older and stronger than he was, but God said: "Man looks at the outside, but God looks at the heart." So God chose David to be the future King of Israel. It was kept a secret, because Saul was already King of Israel, although God wasn't very pleased with him.

Sometimes Saul had black moods. He asked his servants if they knew of anyone who could play the harp and make him feel happier. A servant suggested David who could play the harp beautifully. Saul sent for David who played for him. The King immediately felt better and grew fond of David.

Saul was at war with the Philistines. The armies faced each other across a valley. Every day the Philistines sent their champion into

27

the valley to challenge the Israelites. His name was Goliath and he was a giant. He wore a huge brass helmet and carried a spear as tall as a house. All Saul's soldiers were afraid of him.

One day, David went to visit his brothers in the army. While he was there, Goliath strode into the valley and roared his challenge. All the Israelite soldiers ran away. David was amazed and went to see Saul. "I will fight this giant," he said.

"Don't be ridiculous," said Saul, "you are a boy and he is a mighty warrior."

But David replied: "I killed a lion and a bear when they attacked my father's sheep. Let me fight the giant. God who saved me from the wild animals will help me."

So Saul agreed, lending David his sword; but David wasn't used to it so he put it down and picked five smooth stones from a stream and put them in his shepherd's bag. He also

took his sling, a strip of leather on strings from which he could fire the stones, and his shepherd's stick and went to meet the giant.

When Goliath saw the tiny figure coming towards him he shouted with scorn: "Am I a dog that you come to fight me with a stick?"

But David answered: "You come with sword, spear and shield, but I come with God on my side. He will help me to kill you."

And he ran towards Goliath whirling his sling with a stone in it. He slung the stone and it hit the giant on the forehead, sinking deep into his head. Goliath crashed forward and fell to the ground. David leapt on his body, pulled Goliath's huge sword from its sheath and cut off the head of the giant.

When the Philistine army saw that their champion was dead, they ran away. David became a hero and, when Saul died, he became King of Israel.

DANIEL
IN THE LIONS' DEN

Daniel was a prince, but when he was very young, the great King of Babylon conquered Israel and took Daniel back to Babylon. Daniel did not forget his own country or his own God. He prayed to him every day.

When Daniel grew up he was so clever that King Darius made him a rich and important person.

The Babylonian princes were jealous of Daniel and tricked the King into signing a law, which said that people must only pray to King Darius, otherwise they would be thrown into the lions' den.

Daniel knew the law, but he bravely prayed to God at his open window where everyone could see him. He was arrested and taken before King Darius, who did not want to punish Daniel, but the law was the law. So

Daniel was thrown into the lions' den.

The huge beasts roared and paced up and down as the great stone was rolled from the mouth of the cave. King Darius called after Daniel: "Your God whom you serve will save you from the lions."

Darius spent a miserable night and, in the morning, he rushed to the lions' den and called: "O Daniel, has your God saved you from the lions?"

Daniel replied: "Yes, O King. God sent an angel to shut the lions' mouths because I have done no wrong."

So the den was opened and Daniel was brought out alive because he believed in God.

36

CONTENTS

NEW TESTAMENT

THE BIRTH OF JESUS

Long after Daniel came out of the lions' den, a young woman called Mary lived in a town called Nazareth in Israel. One day, an angel appeared to her and seeing that she was frightened said:

"Don't be afraid, God loves you. He is giving you a special gift – a baby called Jesus who will be the Son of God."

And Mary replied: "I belong to God and will do as he wishes."

Some time after the angel had appeared, Mary went to Bethlehem with Joseph, the man she was going to marry. When they got to the town, all the inns were full; there was nowhere to stay. They were very worried because Mary was about to have her baby.

At last, they found a stable and there, where donkeys and cows lived, Jesus was

born. Mary wrapped him in soft cloths and made a cradle for him in a manger, from which the animals usually fed.

Out on the hills above Bethlehem, shepherds were watching their sheep, guarding them against wild animals. It was a dark night, but suddenly the sky was filled with a strange and brilliant light and an angel appeared. The shepherds were terrified, but the angel said:

"Fear not, I bring you good news. A baby has been born to save the world. Go to Bethlehem and you will find him lying in a manger."

Then the whole sky was filled with angels saying: "Glory be to God in the highest and on earth peace, good will toward men."

The shepherds rushed to Bethlehem and found Jesus. When they had seen him, they told everyone the wonderful story of his birth.

Many miles away in the East, wise men

were studying the stars when they saw a special star which meant that a king had been born. They followed it for miles, to Jerusalem. There they saw King Herod and asked: "Where is the baby that is born to be King of the Jews?"

When Herod heard this he was very angry, because he was King. But being a wicked and cunning man, he told the wise men that he thought the baby was in Bethlehem.

"When you have found him," said Herod, "come back and tell me where he is, so that I too can worship him." But really he wanted to kill the baby.

The wise men followed the star until it stopped over a house in Bethlehem. When they went inside, they saw Mary, Joseph, and Jesus. They knelt down and worshipped Jesus and gave him great treasures of gold, frankincense, and myrrh.

That night, God warned them in a dream

of Herod's evil plans, so they went back to their own country another way.

An angel also warned Joseph of Herod's wickedness and that night the family escaped into Egypt.

When Herod was dead, Mary, Joseph, and Jesus returned to live in Nazareth and Jesus helped Joseph with his carpentry.

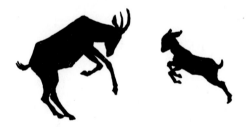

JESUS AND HIS DISCIPLES

When Jesus grew up, he began his important work of teaching people about God. One day, when he was walking beside the lake of Galilee, he saw two fishermen, Simon and Andrew, casting their fishing nets into the sea.

Jesus said to them: "Follow me and I will make you fishers of men." He wanted them to help him teach people about God's love.

Simon and Andrew stopped fishing immediately and followed him. They had only gone a little way, when they saw James and John mending their nets. Jesus called them and they left their nets and followed him.

After Simon, Andrew, James, and John had left everything to follow him, Jesus chose some more followers and helpers. He had twelve disciples in all. He travelled with

them, teaching people about God and healing sick people.

One evening, Jesus rested on the shore while the disciples sailed across Lake Galilee. There was a storm, and as the disciples rowed against the wind and the waves, they saw Jesus walking towards them on the water. Jesus said: "Don't be afraid, it's me."

Simon Peter leapt over the side of the boat to walk to Jesus on the water, but when he was surrounded by the huge waves he was terrified and began to sink.

Jesus stretched out his hand and saved him saying: "Where is your faith, Peter? Why did you doubt me?"

As they climbed back into the boat, the storm stopped and the disciples said to Jesus: "It is true, you are the Son of God."

THE BOY WITH
THE LOAVES AND FISHES

Thousands of people followed Jesus wherever he went. One day, they followed him into the desert. There was nothing for them to eat, but a small boy brought five loaves and two fish to the disciples and said that the crowd could have them.

"How can we feed five thousand people with five loaves and two fish?" asked the disciples.

Jesus told the people to sit down. He took the food and held it up to heaven and blessed it and broke it. Then he gave it to the people.

Everyone had enough to eat and when they collected the scraps, they filled twelve baskets. The people were all amazed, for they had seen a miracle with their own eyes.

JAIRUS' DAUGHTER

There was once a girl, aged about twelve, who fell so ill that she was dying. Her parents were grief stricken. Jairus, her father, begged Jesus to come and save his daughter.

Jesus agreed at once, but before they reached the house, a servant arrived and told them that the little girl was dead.

When they got to the house and went into her room, everyone was crying. "Don't cry," said Jesus, "she isn't dead, she's asleep."

They did not believe him, so he sent everyone away. He took the little girl's hand and said: "Little girl, get up."

She sat up and asked for some food. Her parents, amazed and overjoyed, thanked Jesus for saving their daughter.

HOW JESUS DIED

Jesus decided to go to Jerusalem, the capital city. His disciples found him a donkey to ride and they set out. As they went, crowds of people lined the streets and cheered "Hosanna". They threw palm leaves in front of the donkey; it was a happy procession.

But the leaders of the synagogue, the Jewish church, were jealous and afraid of Jesus because he was so popular, and they plotted to kill him.

One of the disciples, Judas, was disappointed that Jesus had not overthrown the Romans who ruled Israel at the time, so he went to the leaders of the synagogue and offered to tell them where they could arrest Jesus. He betrayed Jesus for thirty pieces of silver.

One evening, Jesus went with his disciples

to the Garden of Gethsemane to pray. "Oh my Father," he prayed, "do not let me suffer and die, but your will, not mine, be done."

Suddenly, they were surrounded by a huge crowd of soldiers and servants of Caiaphas the high priest, carrying lanterns, swords, and sticks.

They bound Jesus and took him before Caiaphas, who accused Jesus of wanting to lead a rebellion against the Romans. Caiaphas sent him to Pontius Pilate, the Roman Governor.

Pilate questioned Jesus, but could find him guilty of no crime. He wanted to release him because he knew that the Jewish priests were jealous of Jesus. But the priests stirred up the crowd in the street saying that Jesus was a trouble maker and the crowd roared: "Crucify him, crucify him."

Pilate, fearing a riot, sentenced Jesus to be crucified to death.

The Roman soldiers beat Jesus and pushed a crown of thorns on his head. Then they made him carry a huge wooden cross to a hill called Golgotha. There they nailed him to the cross.

Jesus said: "Father forgive them, they do not know what they do."

After much suffering Jesus died saying: "Father, I give my spirit into your hands."

His friends wrapped his body in linen, put it in a cave tomb, and rolled a great stone over the entrance.

THE RESURRECTION

A day passed, and early the next morning Mary Magdalene, Mary mother of Thomas, and Salome went to the tomb in the garden. They found that the great stone had been rolled away and the body of Jesus had gone. Only the linen cloth was left.

As the women wept, an angel appeared. "Don't be afraid," said the angel, "Jesus has risen from the dead. Go and tell the disciples."

Mary Magdalene stayed, weeping. She did not believe the angel. A man she thought was the gardener asked her why she was crying.

"Please," said Mary, "if you have taken my Lord's body, tell me where he is."

The man said: "Mary". And she knew it was Jesus who stood before her – alive.

THE MAN BY THE LAKE

The disciples found it hard to believe that Jesus was alive again. One night they went fishing, but by morning they had caught nothing. As they stood in their boat, a voice came across the water. It was a man standing on the shore. They could not see his face, but he called again: "Cast your nets on the right side of the boat."

The disciples did, and their nets filled with fish. John said to Peter: "It is the Lord."

Peter immediately jumped into the water and waded ashore where he saw that Jesus had lit a fire and was baking bread and fish. The other disciples followed, and they ate breakfast with Jesus.

JESUS GOES TO HEAVEN

Jesus appeared to his disciples and friends several times after he had risen from the dead.

The last time they saw him he took them to a mountain and said to them: "You must travel to every corner of the earth and tell people about God's love. I will be with you always, even to the end of the world."

Then he blessed them, and as he did a golden cloud floated over him. Jesus was drawn up by the cloud to heaven to be by the side of God, his father.